better together*

*This book is best read together, grownup and kid.

 akidsco.com

a
kids
book
about

a kids book about ✓OTING

by Next Up

A Kids Co.
Editor Denise Morales Soto
Designer Duke Stebbins
Creative Director Rick DeLucco
Studio Manager Kenya Feldes
Sales Director Melanie Wilkins
Head of Books Jennifer Goldstein
CEO and Founder Jelani Memory

DK
Editor Emma Roberts
Senior Production Editor Jennifer Murray
Senior Production Controller Louise Minihane
Senior Acquisitions Editor Katy Flint
Acquisitions Project Editor Sara Forster
Managing Art Editor Vicky Short
Publishing Director Mark Searle
DK would like to thank Jamia Wilson

This American Edition, 2024
Published in the United States by DK Publishing
1745 Broadway, 20th Floor, New York, NY 10019

DK, a Division of Penguin Random House LLC
Text and design copyright © 2020 by A Kids Book About, Inc.
Author photograph © Aubrie Pick
A Kids Book About, Kids Are Ready, and the colophon 'a' are trademarks of A Kids Book About, Inc.
24 25 26 27 10 9 8 7 6 5 4 3 2 1
001-344031-Sep/2024

A catalog record for this book is available from the Library of Congress.
ISBN: 978-0-5939-5717-2

DK books are available at special discounts when purchased in bulk for
sales promotions, premiums, fund-raising, or educational use. For details, contact:
DK Publishing Special Markets, 1745 Broadway, 20th Floor, New York, NY 10019, or SpecialSales@dk.com

Printed and bound in China

www.dk.com

akidsco.com

For the youth of America,
keep fighting for voting rights.

Foreword

by Jamia Wilson

Author, publisher, movement builder, and feminist activist

As a child, I eagerly awaited Sunday tea-times when my mother, Freda, would share tales of bravery and resilience. One story deeply moved me, and I asked to hear it repeatedly. It was the story of my grandfather Albert, who was born in South Carolina in 1911 when segregation was the law of the land in the American South. Despite the harsh circumstances, he traveled the South to register and engage voters and pave the way for change, decades before the 1965 Voting Rights Act forbade states from blocking voters of color from the ballot box by using discriminatory tactics.

During our teas, I learned about the value of voting, protecting our access to it, and doing the work to make sure everyone is educated about their voting rights, has a fair shot at the ballot box, and has a chance to be counted.

As you and the kid you're reading with turn the pages of this book, I encourage you to use what's inside to reflect on how you see yourselves exercising your right to be heard, taking a stand for the causes and ideas that matter to you, and the value of helping others who may need help to be heard too. Your kid may not have the legal right to vote for elected office yet, but when the time comes, these conversations will help them be ready to make a difference for the leaders and causes that inspire them.

Jamia

Intro
for grownups

Voting is deeply important, and we often underestimate its power. Through voting, we decide which people and ideas mold and influence our day-to-day lives. Which is why it's so crucial that we not only understand what voting is, but also its history.

Young people are imaginative and there is no end to their potential. So when you teach kids about voting, and about the honor, privilege, and responsibility of being able to vote, they can discover their role in creating solutions to the problems we face. And importantly, they can imagine what voting can be when it's their turn to make the decisions.

The younger people are when they develop their civic habits, the more likely they are to become lifelong voters. We hope that this book will serve as a first step toward that lifelong practice.

Are there any words or ideas that you don't understand? Check the back of the book for a page of definitions.

HELLO!

We are a group of young people who care about making positive changes in the world.

One of the ways we do
that is by helping young people
(like you!) learn more about

VOTING.

But we've already gotten
ahead of ourselves…

You probably want to
know what voting is!

Voting is how you show your
support for a person or idea.
You do this with something
called a **VOTE.**

A **vote**, simply put, is a record of your *choice* for something or someone.

Like, should we have pizza for dinner?

YES ■

NO ■

WHAT
do people vote
FOR ?

Things like ideas, laws, how money is spent, and even who will be president.

HOW?

do we vote?

This depends on where you live.

People can vote in person by filling in an oval, square, or other shape on a piece of paper, or on a computer.

It is also possible to vote early (before election day), by mail, or by dropping off your completed ballot at a designated location.

Currently, every state except North Dakota requires voters to register before they vote.

WHO?

gets to vote?

Well, that's a little more complicated...

When our country,
the United States of America,
was founded, only some people
were allowed to vote.

Let us explain...

Before the USA existed,
many European countries used
America for land, wealth, and power.
That is called colonialism.

But there were people
who already lived in America,
who today we call **Indigenous people**.

The Indigenous peoples living in
America were forced from their lands,
which were sacred to them, and many
were even *killed*.

And African people were brutally captured, sold, taken far from their homes and families, and forced into chattel slavery in America.

Chattel slavery is one of the worst things that has ever happened in human history; it is when a human being is considered the property of another person.

After a while, the people from Europe wanted even more power...

...so they created their own country,
the United States of America,
on the land of the Indigenous peoples.

They generally ignored the rich voting history of peoples like those in the Haudenosaunee Confederacy,* and instead made their own rules and decided who got to vote on them.

*Look it up, it's really cool!

To do this, in 1789 they* wrote
a document called **the Constitution**.

The Constitution laid out the laws
of the land that everyone had to follow.
It also said who could vote.

* white European men

Can you guess who got the

RIGHT

TO VOTE

as granted in the Constitution?

WHITE

MEN

...who had been given the right and freedom to own land and pay taxes.

This was only around **6%** of all the people in the country at the time.

If you were a grownup in 1789,
would **you** have been allowed to vote?

How about your **best friend**?
Your **teacher**?
Your **parents**?

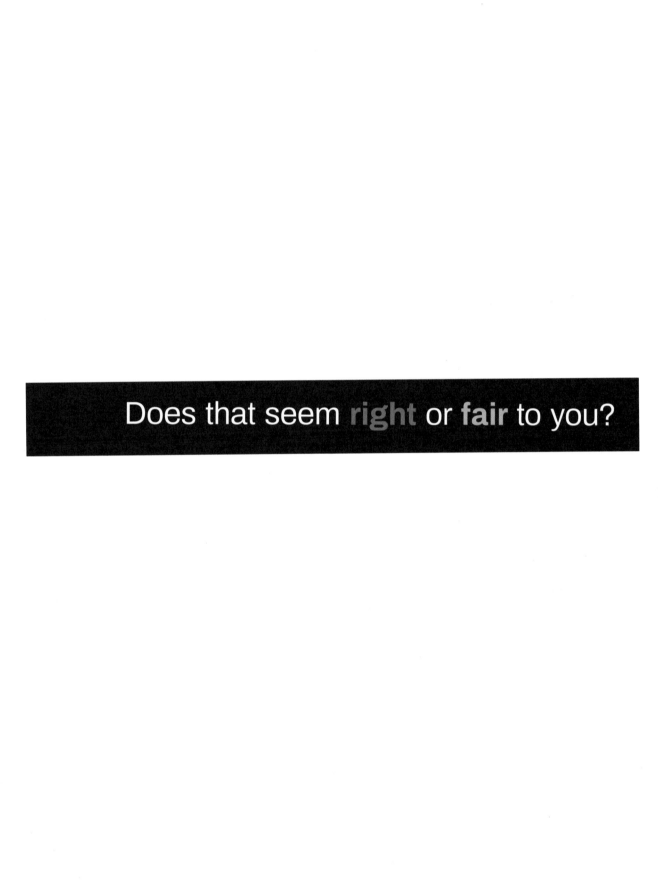

Does that seem **right** or **fair** to you?

Many people in our country haven't been able to vote because of their:

RACE

AGE

GENDER

RELIGION

LITERACY

LACK OF WEALTH

LANGUAGE

CITIZENSHIP

or because they have

A DISABILITY.

BUT
WHO CAN VOTE
HAS CHANGED
OVER TIME...

1870

It wasn't until almost *100 years* after the Constitution was written that Black men got the right to vote.

1920

50 years after that, white women were allowed to vote.

1924

Soon after, a new law was made that gave Indigenous people citizenship and the right to vote, but many states kept them from voting until **1957**.

Even after all of this, it still didn't mean
that **every** Black man, white woman,
and Indigenous person got the right to vote.

A lot of them were still left out.

Eventually,
more groups of people got to vote, like in..........

1952 Asian people gained citizenship and the right to vote.

1965 The Voting Rights Act said there couldn't be any barriers to **ANYONE** voting (in theory). This is when all Black women finally gained the right to vote.

1970 The age for voting changed from 21 to **18**.

1975 **Latinx people** who couldn't read English gained the right to vote using Spanish-language ballots.

1990 The Americans with Disabilities Act ensured that **individuals with disabilities** could vote.

We want you to pause
and think about all of this for a minute.

STOP.
BREATHE.
REFLECT.

Does it seem right to you that it took
so long for so many people
to get a chance to vote?

We think it's

OUTRAGEOUS

UNFAIR

and simply

NOT RIGHT.

Still not everyone can vote,
but now more people than *ever* can.

That makes us

HOPEFUL,

because it shows that things can change.

In the future, we hope that even **MORE** people will have the right to vote.

HOW?

Through new **laws**, the **people** we elect, the decisions of the **government**, and people using their voices and working together to make change happen.

And how do *new laws* and *governments* get formed?

iNG

There are lots of different things you'll get to vote for when you're a grownup.

Like who is President of the United States,

who the mayor of your city is,

and *so many more things, like......*

PARKS

SCHOOLS

JUDGES

SENATORS

PLAYGROUNDS

RULE CHANGES

GOVERNORS

SHERIFFS

MONEY

AND ON

AND ON

AND ON.

Voting happens all the time and each time is for something different.

Almost **every year**
we vote for local things.

Every **4 years**
we vote for a president.

Every **6 years**
we vote for our
United States senators.

Voting is one of the most

IMPORTANT

things you can do.

It's not just using your voice;
it's something even more special......

YOUR

POW

VER.

Yes, you are **powerful**.

When you vote, you use your power for what you believe in.

Whether it's an **idea,**

or **person,**

or **movement.**

When you get to vote,
it will be because many people
fought to give you that right.

When we vote, individual voices come together to make a bigger

SOUND.

voting allows us to advocate
for people and issues we believe in.

It doesn't just happen with **1** vote, but with man
ny many many many many many many mar
ny many many **many** many many many mar
ny many **many** many many many many **many** mar
ny **many** many **many** many many many **many** mar
ny many **many** many **many** many **many** many mar
ny many many many many many many **many** mar
ny many **many** many many **many** many many mar
ny **many** many many **many** many many **many** mar
ny many **many** many **many** many many **many** mar

many many many many many many many many many
many many many many many many many many many many
many many many many many many many many many many
many many many many many many many many many many
many many many many many many many many many many
many many many many many many many many many many
many many many many many many many many many man
many many many many many many many many many man
many many many many many many many many many man
many many many many many many many many many man

Which means **your vote**
(eventually, when you can)

is *so important.*

Because sometimes something wins by just **1** vote,
or **7**,
or **3000**.

So your vote matters!

But sadly, not everyone who can vote, does.

For example, during big elections, like for the president, only about 50% of people in America who can vote *do* vote.

So what will you do?

WILL YOU:

Use your voice

YES ☐

NO ☐

Stand up for what you believe in

YES ☐

NO ☐

Vote

YES ☐

NO ☐

?

Outro
for grownups

Now that you've finished this book—what's next?

Share your personal stories about voting with the kid you're reading with. What are the positive experiences you've had? Have you ever faced any challenges to casting your ballot?

Encourage them to practice using their voice for change. That could be at home, or in school, sports, groups, or clubs. Consider running as a candidate for office in one of these places.

Kids are so smart. The solutions to the world's problems are within their minds, waiting to be discovered. So encourage their ideas. Let them think and dream and ask questions and wonder how things could be better.

Remind them that they have a voice, they have a right, and they have the power to decide on the future they want to see.

About The Authors

Kids have a right to make decisions about the world in which they live and the future they will inherit. At Next Up, we support youth in order to make lasting social change through grassroots organizing, centering the leadership of Black youth, Indigenous youth, and other youth of color, and youth who are the most impacted by the issues we face.

By investing in youth movements, Next Up has won major victories for voting rights, developed new generations of young leaders, and shifted systems of power. We operate with the knowledge that young people can be trusted with power—not as "future leaders" but as leaders of today.

Contributions to this book made by:
*Amanda Squiemphen-Yazzie, Devin Ruiz,
Amira Tripp Folsom, Izzy Dacones-Rowland,
Isabela Villarreal, and Samantha Gladu.*

 @nextuporegon   @nextuporegon   nextuporegon.org

DEFINITIONS:

ACT
Also known as a law or rule.

ADVOCATE
To speak for or defend a cause.

BALLOT
A means of voting which is private. The vote is kept confidential, or, secret. The word ballot can refer to the things being voted on, and also the way the vote is cast: most usually on a piece of paper, or on a voting machine.

CITIZENSHIP
The position of being recognized by the law as a member of a country.

GOVERNMENT
People who have the authority to make decisions for a community. There are lots of people in government, including at a federal (USA), state, county, city, tribal, and territorial level.

GOVERNOR
The top lawmaker in a state.

JUDGE
A person who makes decisions about how laws are carried out.

LAW
A rule.

MAYOR
The top lawmaker in a city.

MOVEMENT
When people work together to create change in government policy or social values.

RACE
An idea not based on scientific principles and a social label that groups people based on physical and cultural qualities.

SENATOR
A member of the Senate, which is a group that is focused on protecting the good of the country.

SHERIFF
A person who makes sure laws are being followed.

Made to empower.

a kids book about racism
by Jelani Memory

a kids book about ANXIETY
by Ross Szabo

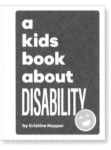
a kids book about DISABILITY
by Kristine Napper

a kids book about IMAGINATION
by LEVAR BURTON

a kids book about belonging
by Kevin Carroll

a kids book about failyure
by Dr. Laymon Hicks

a kids book about GRATITUDE
by Ben Kenyon

a kids book about LIFE ONLINE
by Dave S. Anderson & Blake Fleischacker

a kids book about body image
by Rebecca Alexander

a kids book about IMMIGRATION
by MJ Calderon

a kids book about EMPATHY
by Daron K. Roberts

a kids book about GENDER
by Dale Mueller

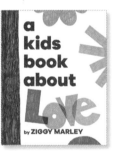
a kids book about Love
by ZIGGY MARLEY

a kids book about EQUALITY
by BILLIE JEAN KING

a kids book about MONEY
by Adam Stramwasser

a kids book about FEMINISM
by Emma McIlroy

a kids book about adventure
by Dr. Ben Tortin

a kids book about CLIMATE CHANGE
by Zonagee Artis Olivia Greenspan

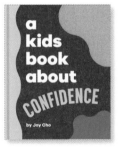
a kids book about CONFIDENCE
by Joy Cho

a kids book about BEING NONBINARY
by Hunter Chinn-Raicht
in partnership with The Gender Cool Project

Discover more at akidsco.com